The Conflict That Creates

Poems by Antony V. Plocido

Luchador Press

Big Tuna, TX

Copyright © Antony V. Plocido, 2021
First Edition: 1 3 5 7 9 10 8 6 4 2
ISBN: 978-1-952411-50-2
LCCN: 2021931290

Cover art: "Portal," Jenny Hahn
(https://www.jennyhahnart.com/)
Author photos: Tony Plocido
Artist Website: www.mentalvalley.com
Instagram: @mentalvalley

Acknowledgments:

"Precipitation" was originally published in *Broad Strokes: Talking Stick* Volume 28 by Jackpine Writers' Bloc, Inc. Page 71.

"Numb" was originally published in *Broad Strokes: Talking Stick* Volume 28 by Jackpine Writers' Bloc, Inc. Page 155.

"Awakened" was originally published in *The Moccasin: Family Reunion* by The League of MN Poets (mnpoets. org). Page 82.

"Awakened" then appeared in *Spectra: Poems of Growth Told Through the Chakras* by Err Minneapolis Art Collective. Page 18.

TABLE OF CONTENTS

I dedicate this book to all of the poetry community that
has supported me and all of the events I put together.
Poets, friends, and family, thank you so much!

I would also like to thank Jas Abramowitz, Namdi
Alexander, Brett Elizabeth Jenkins, Brian Baumgart, and
Ashley Vernes Cardona for helping with the editing some
of these pieces.

Thank you to Charlie Curry, Ashley Vernes Cardona &
Brett Elizabeth Jenkins for editing this book.   You take my
madness and make it readable.

For those of us who survived 2020, I hope we never have
another year like it.

~ Antony V. Plocido

...if you want to start thinking on a "universe" scale, we are technically insignificant; but there's no reason to live your life thinking that.

-Anonymous

A Life with Poetry

There are so many times
when life is thought in the way of poetry.
Metaphors are water to drink.
Similes are like the rooms where I live.
They're not always great but
they're home.
Every breeze has an air of
something greater. As though
I may elevate
you.
Me.
Literarily.

I write these thoughts down
for your consumption.
You looked like you needed to eat.

So here, let me
share this with you—
these tercets on my tongue, these free verse phrases
plucked and peeled by frantic fingers;
there's stanza enough for
all of us.

We say grace. It sounds like an agreement,

Can't we all appreciate a little alliteration?

Don't we all want to go to bed beside the words that
remind us we are real?

Don't we want to wake up to the ideas
that light our day?
Make us understand that the night isn't evil.
It's where the sonnets are softened.
Turned into paintings of people that could have only been
understood
through characters on a page.

A picture is worth a thousand words but
with poetry there is no shortage of words.
We have found the economy of speech and we present it to you
in front of microphones no one paid to see,
in books no one cared to buy, and
in parks.
Where if one person heard,
the process had purpose.

Then, it had substance.

*Warning: If you ever find anything with poetry written on it and don't pick it up,
you are messing with the universe. Art is best when it falls into your lap.*

Arts & Crafts

It isn't Valentine's Day
that crushes you
to a fine powder;
its only real use
is to add water and
hope your heart grows back.

Instead it creates a hard plaster
that maybe you could use
to fix the hole in the wall.
The one you named after her,
even though it was there
when you moved in.

Maybe with a little more water
from tears (or
the shower you've been sitting in
producing said tears)
you can make clay.

You can then mold that
into a shape.
If not a heart,
something that makes you feel
like you are loved.

Note: Valentine's Day is the worst.

Awakened

If you can't find time
in the middle of the night,
to build yourself up
when no one is watching;
you will notice the deterioration.
The slow melt of time.

I am not saying it will get better.
I don't know if it will.
I do know that is *can* get better.

They say, "There's always a light
at the end of the tunnel."
But it's not at the end of the tunnel.
The light is
everywhere
but the tunnel.
Stay out of the tunnel.

Tell yourself that every wrinkle
is a story
not a curse.

Clean the mirror
before you use it.
Your reflection has earned that much.

You're up now.
The wee hours
are when people can feel small. But
you're a giant in your world.
Every last bit of you
deserves to be awakened.

Baptize

splash
sink
watch the ripples of light
the swim of fish
the bottom's not far
the bottom's not good
though the sand provides
comfort

when the need for air
surpasses the need
for peace
I'll find my way up
again
then

splash

the water
doesn't take away my sins
it makes them feel
cleaner

the descent

a necessary cycle

the wash

the wait

ascent

breathe

*Note: Transgressions are wet clothes. If you keep wearing them,
you'll chafe.*

Breaking and Entering

I presented myself as option.

I wanted to break into
her crowded noise.
She had two choices:
Either a thousand nervous nights alone, or
a thousand herded kids at home.
Hyperbole aside,
she knows an absence of freedom.
She might run.
She's definitely done.

She swallows poison nightly
she doesn't want to fight me or
digest the grief and I
offer no relief.
Only an elixir.
I believe I can fix her.
Mix her emotions
into something she can maintain.
It becomes a hangover
and over,
and over.

Without "drive" inside her,
she resides here
in her own mind and
it is lonely.

If only I didn't love her.
If only I could hover above her and
pick off
bad thoughts
before they had a chance to land.

As it stands,
I'm not her hero.
I'm less than zero on a
scale from one to ten.
I'm categorized as "men"
followed closely with a sigh and
I can't really argue. But
I'd really like to.

The old tropes that gave us hope like,
"Nope, I'm not one of them." or
"You can't put me in with him."
Truth is, I've hurt people too.
Maybe not you but
my slate isn't clean.
I've been mean to those
who chose to love me.

There was no one
to hover above me and
pick off those bad thoughts.
There never is.
I'm no longer sure
what my point is.

Maybe it's that
we always want
to be everything to those we love.
Whether it be spouse or kids.
Until we realize what everything
is.
Then the mountain grows taller than our sight goes.

No!
Shit. Where did I go?

I stopped talking about her
a minute ago.
This became about me
a second ago.
I also seemed to have walked away.

Who's left to say
that I even tried to break into
her crowded noise?

She won't have to choose
if there isn't a choice.

Warning: Never assume someone else is weak. They might be your last support.

Bright

Some of what I wrote
was just an effigy of you.
I meant to burn those poems.

I was unable
to bring fire to you.
Maybe my judgements
were too cold.

So now you're just a
straw doll and
metaphors I can't get away from.

Note: This poem came to me after listening to Uncle Tupelo's version of "Effigy." Though this poem is about a completely different thing, though strangely apropos to sing, "Who we burnin'? Who we burnin'? in your head."

Childish Thoughts on
Adult Situations

I used to think that
I took the path of least resistance.

I've learned a lot of things
in the last ten years.
Not the least of which was
I was wrong about that.

I'm always full sails,
wrong direction,
on a windy day.

There are so many windy days.

Being an adult,
most of the time,
is the perfect storm. And
I'm always wearing the wrong shoes.

Warning: "Everybody wants the path of least resistance but the path of least resistance is what makes the river crooked!" ~Utah Phillips or Adulting is hard.

Craftsman / Artist

I could build a table.
The legs would be straight.
The top would be flat-ish.
This wouldn't make me a carpenter.
In fact, it would be
more like art.

Separating craftsman
from artist
is a poor thing to do.
As though the craftsman's work
should be viewed.
Admired and not used.

But I can turn nouns
into nails.
Verbs into cuttings.
Working with boards
of abstract ideas.

When I have finished my table,
sanded with simile,
planed with metaphor,
topped with a stain
of all of the stuff floating through my head,
we will eat a meal.

Even if it has a slight slant,
a way of looking;
if some things slide away
that's okay.
They probably weren't worth
keeping in front of you anyway.

Note: I once had an assignment to build a square, wooden box. Even that ended up to be more of a rectangle/trapezoid-type thing. Do what you can. That's all that's ever really required.

Daggers

Did he decide to leave?
That night your fire
got so hot
that all respect had melted?

That night you said
all the things
you said you'd never say
in front of the children?

Did he come back
still looking for answers?
Still wanting to hear
the rest of the story?

He did.

The daggers all missed their mark.
He's known your warmth.
He is oblivious
to your heat.

Warning: Take note of your attitude before they get tired of dodging.

Dim Light

The moon was so full,
I could see it
reflecting
in her hair.

She was always good
at collecting the light.
I found I could see better
when she was near.

This, of course,
is how I noticed the cracks.
It's amazing what you can
get away with in dim light.

Note: If you know the line that I borrowed from Dessa. Good for you.

Fairy Tales

I want a lasting relationship
with my country.
I want to feel like patriotism
is important.
I want to know
that everyone is ok where they are.
I want to see beauty
in every direction I look.
Even down.
I want to hear
the soft sigh of relief
as the people finally stand up.
But
magic isn't real.
Boundaries are guesses. And
we just aren't equipped,
as people,
to come together.

*Warning: Your description of patriotism isn't necessarily correct. Stop
pretending you know.*

How Water Sees the Stone

Does she have to be
the sea?
Her fluidity
leaves me
nowhere to stand.
A man without a shore.
This hand
could use four more
hands that can catch her. And
I'm sure she doesn't care
or notice.

She just floats this idea
of freedom.
A grand scale and
a wee sum
all swirled together.

It seems like forever
to get to her
particular
part of the ocean.
Earth bound and hopin'.
Closed thoughts opened the way
for this pattern.

I had earned her trust
and then thrust my insecurities
into her pocket.

They weighted her feet and
her eye sockets.
And I could have stopped it.

I chose to dissent.
To disagree.
Essentially to flee
my responsibilities and
she stayed
here
floating in a sea of fear.

Riding the waves and
the tide
choosing not to hide
from her detractors.
Choosing to fight her attackers.
Choosing to take back and
stack the deck in her favor.

Stupid of me
to try to be a savior.
When all I could do is stand and
only when there was land.

The hand I held out
was only doubt,
in the form of a palm.

She chooses calm.

There simply no way to argue.

Note: The rock can only temporarily hold back the water. Water will win.

Legacy

There isn't time for this.
Dark, black emotions and
incessant chatter about lines.
Where we should stand
in relation to them.

Opinions weigh more
when you're dead.
Those who cared
will carry them through time for you.
Leaving pieces of your mind
on people you've never met.

Your message,
which didn't matter
in the first place,
is now an estimate
of your original emotion.

For the sake of clarity and
distinguished thought:
because your legacy
will never be your history.
It might just be better
to shut the fuck up.

*Warning: To the targets of this poem: most of us are tired of your shit.
Some will not keep their fatigue to themselves.*

Lydia

They named the new baby giraffe
Lydia.
I cried.

That would have been your name.
Had I lived my life differently,

I would have taken you to the zoo.
We could have laughed about
how you shared your name
with the new baby giraffe.

My regrets
feel like prayers.
New life
should not feel like loss.

Note: I have always wanted kids. The more time that ticks on without them weighs me down more. I feel unending grief for the parents who don't give all the love to their children. Those parents who don't realize how lucky they are.

Morning

My form flies low in the morning.
I'm not grounded.
That's both good and
bad.

Since turning 40,
every morning is a milestone.
I open the curtains and
see the world wakes with me.

I'm sad to know
that the day
this will no longer be true
will be unknown to me.

Warning: You rarely get to know the day you will be dying. Make sure you always have your shit together.

Numb

Then you broke.
You were told so many times
that your eyes got black.
From crying,
not from pain.
Which was worse than the punches.

Sadness is water in a drain.
It swirls out and
then the hurt stops.

Numb.
The feeling of not feeling.

If it had some Zen,
it might be useful. But
it isn't tranquility.
It's tedium.

Find your glue.
The duct tape for this dilemma.
Because sticks and stones
may break your bones, but
that only matters if you can feel them.

*Note: Don't stop in the middle of the intersection. Something is going
to hit you.*

Observing Religion

She says she prays.
Kneels down.
Talks to God.
She's been searching for forgiveness.

If God doesn't forgive her
she has no reason to stop.
If he does,
she can finally get off her knees.
She doesn't know life
without dogma.

She'll eat the cracker,
drink the wine,
until Christ finally shows.
Helps her up,
wipes his body and blood
from her lips and
convinces her that forgiveness came
as soon as she asked.

I think
life is harder
when you need a savior.

*Warning: Religion is based on Earth. Earth is unimportant to the universe.
This means religion at best is incomplete and at worst irrelevant.*

Precipitation

There was often sadness
at the ends of her sentences.
It sounded like rain
coming through the roof.
It could have been relaxing
if there wasn't a slow destruction
happening.

She liked to hold my hand
when she spoke of
stubborn subjects
like love
or yesterday.
She said it kept her from drifting.

I would catch her drift,
so I would speak of
center lines,
lanes and
how to drop this nonsense.
I mean, we had to share this road.

I used to dream
that she would talk to me.

Back before I knew

how much her accent

would affect me.

Like this weather.

I wanted to stay dry, but

that's not what rain does.

Note: This is the second poem where I refer to women as water.
I mean, if you were looking for a running metaphor.

Regret

I wandered
low
to the bottom
of the last thing I recognized.
What I saw was the lack of anything to see.
There has never been less.

This must be
what your last moments will feel like.
In that moment,
when you can no longer hear,
but your mind hasn't
quite sauntered away.

It must sound
like the ocean.
There must be waves
of regret.
Humans
are so prone to regret.
We use it as a cane
to keep us on our feet.

I have had
a lot of spare time
in my busy schedule
to study these
molecules of misused moments.

These semblances
of turning left
when I should have stayed right.
I've learned
that there wasn't
a "right" to turn.
This is not to say
there is destiny.
Just that what you did
is done.
Undone is
unobtainable.

So, the next time
you sleep,
maybe she's there or
maybe you're alone,
pick a direction
that isn't backwards.
Forward
is the only option
left to those
who don't want to sit
in this empty room.

The one with the ocean.

Warning: By the time you turn 40 you realize that learning to deal with regret, in a healthy way, is one of those things you'll wish you had learned when you were young.

Ruling

Did you know there is more time
between the Pyramids being built and
Cleopatra's rule,
then there is
between Cleopatra and
me,
now.

Even that doesn't begin to explain
the roots of humanity. But
it does give an idea
how long people have
controlled people.

I don't have a solution.
I'm just sad
that I'm part of the question.

Note: This is my fun fact at parties. I guess I'll have to find another one.

See

You know sadness.
I have seen it.
All of the times you reached
to the top shelf
to find booze
or your soul.
I've seen it.

When you wake
in the morning,
or mid-afternoon,
do you even see the sun?
I've seen it.
It traveled so very far
to find you.
Its reflection on your tears
is gorgeous.
You should see it.

Do not mistake me.
I'm not here to make you better.
I just miss your smile.
I've seen it
in my latest recollections.
I've seen it
every time I've felt
alone in my skin.

No one can tell you
to calm down.
No one can tell you
to be happy.
I've seen how little effect
that can have.
Especially in this darkness
where you can't see.

Before you fade
completely
look at me.
See your past.
Tell me you remember.
Because this isn't a love letter.
This a photograph.
The only one I ever need you to ____

*Warning: The blank at the end of the poem is a gift for you to fill in.
If you can't figure it out, please consult a thesaurus or ask one of the
English majors you know.*

Sensing

It's oh so quiet.
I hear to entertain.
I can hear the static
in the universe.
The massless buzz
that has bounded across the black and
rotates around my ears.
Or
I have listened to too much loud music and
now I am cursed with tinnitus.

The oven timer goes off
and
I'm hungry.

I eat to live.
Life feeds on life
takes new meaning in isolation.
The bumps on my tongue may have receded.
Every flavor feels distant
though the burn is real.

Moments pass and
the plate empties.

I see to learn.
I see from a distance
friends on a screen.

The colors are wrong.
Faces aren't looking at me.
The light isn't reflecting
what my memories reflect.

The smell is different.
The picture of friends
in the woods
recalls the scent of pine and
openness.

I smell to decide
the safety of my surroundings.
This place is dust and
desolation.
Physically safe.
Mentally a Thunderdome of thought.
This scent is free of being.

No other being exists here.
Touch is the real determination
of existence.

I feel so that I know I'm not alone.
I haven't felt touch in too long.
My skin cells
have begun reaching for it.
They stretch until
their metaphorical muscles are pulled.

They attempt to reach out through
phone calls and correspondence.
A breeze brings my head around
hoping to see a face.
Even if danger follows close.

My eyes. My tongue. My nose. My skin.
My ears all agree.
It's oh so quiet.

Note: The pandemic hit me pretty hard. I am a social introvert. I like my home/alone time but I need people too. I have needed a hug for months at time of writing this. The COVID-19 pandemic of 2020 will either go down as the thing that drove us together (as we stayed separate) or the thing that drove you insane.

Spectrums

What happened to spectrums?
Apathy - Activism
Sadness - Glee
Healthy - Dying

All we know
is that the ends are bad.
We float in the middle.
Feeling righteousness
or guilt.
No one is entitled
to an opinion
outside their friend circle.

Unless the goal is
to obtain a new circle.

Conversation has died.
Spectrums have died
They were buried.
Together.
Given a funeral.
Eulogies were spoken with picket signs.
Crying was allowed
but considered a form of protest.

My opinion
was at that funeral.
It stood 15 paces away,
against a tree,
watching Chaos lower the coffin.
Quiet.

We hear calls
to be involved. But
it's all or nothing.
Some of us are left with
fear.
Frozen.

I love you but
I'm not going to talk about this with you.

I guess we can hope
that these are not our final words.

Warning: Cancel culture is, was, and will always be bad. Say it loud and repeat. The villains should be punished; but we cancel too quickly. If the person who wronged has no interest or intent of making themselves better, then fine. See ya! But if they want to heal or change, then we need to listen. That's not to say crimes shouldn't be punished. It's to say that after, rehabilitation should be allowed.

Story

I lost every part of you.
It was subtle.

First
it was the real color of your lips.
It was the one thing
always made up.
A lie.

Second
were the gentle lines
of your hands.
They told your story
in quiet ways.
A tale.

Third
was your voice.
It's been so long
that I can't remember
pitch or timbre,
tone or tempo.
A silence.

Now you're just memory.

No lips or lines.

No scent or sound.

Simply put

a story.

*Note: You'll forget one or two of them. Don't beat yourself up over it.
Remember what you can but most people don't have to write about
a book about their lives.*

Stuck

You won't fault me
if I no longer find this amusing.
My levity left
when you did.

The first time.

I know my body can't say no.
You'll no longer
get the same response
from my face.

The Detective

Failure finds me.
It's good at
breaking down the clues,
narrowing the suspects, and
uncovering my location.

It has to be exhausting,
always seeking me out.
Never keeping me for long because
I was born ready for it and
I'm a slippery son of a bitch.

Note: Keep searching. Keep moving. Don't let it find you.

The Remainder of Our Time

(for Rev. Jen)

I read to you.
I knew the darkness had come but
I had faith your ears still
functioned.
I tried to read the poems
that painted pictures.

I didn't want you to be scared.

You were always the woman
that had a handle on things; but
nonetheless
the metaphors were big.

Vivid.

Clear.

My eyes were not.
Reading to you,
that day,
was almost as hard
as saying goodbye.

Almost.

Warning: Don't miss those chances to say goodbye.
They only come once.

Treats

What's telling you
the thoughts
that you shouldn't be having?

Telling you that
millions of years of evolution
doesn't explain
why thinking of me
tastes like caramel.

The melted butter.
The sugar.
A bit
salty.

Why I represent all the things
you let linger
in your mouth.

Note: If this piece made you feel a bit randy go find that lover of yours and give them a squeeze in the first place that comes to mind.

Trolls Regenerate Unless
You Burn Them

I'm fucking fascinating, man.
I'm also right.
I'm going to use random grammatical symbols
as swear words
because I believe it means
I'm kinder than you.
I am the political poster.
The Facebook Educator.

Please don't mistake me
for the people who research a topic.

Squares.

Or the people
who actually lived through the thing
I'm preaching about.

Whiners.

I am the righteous.
I have been given the gifts of God and
the internet
to educate you poor, peon fools.
I am the voice of my followers.
Facebook calls them my friends but
we know they salivate for my next post.

My next jab.
My next "screw those liberal assholes and
those red dipshits."
I'm inventing a new side.

If you can read this post
then you can feel this post.
Innuendo aside,
that's all I really needed from a day.

Send.
Breathe.
Put on a smile for the aftermath.

Warning: This poem was a work of satire. If you feel the need to cancel me over this piece (or unfriend), I encourage you to look up the meaning of the word "satire."

Wander

We've found life
in this desolation.

My mind has surprisingly little water.

Yet, we wander on.
You were at the beginning.
We strolled hand in hand.
The more we spoke
the less substance I had
for you.

My ambitions weren't interesting.
I know this,
now.
Your ambitions were everything.

As I listened to you speak,
I felt the drift.
I could feel that
you were chasing your dreams;

but to me
it just looked like
you were running away.

Note: People will tell you who they are. Pay attention.

What He Says to Her

(a poem from Will to Jenn)

There is something weird,
or impossible,
about this.
Like having three halves of something.
Like finding Jimmy Hoffa
in King Tut's tomb.
It works, though.

There's life and love here.
It's growing
where I thought the earth was salted.
It's filling me up. But
not like I'm sinking.
More like a balloon.

The city looks wonderful from up here.
The lights are all on and
I hear music.
The city that has shown me darkness.
The city where my address
was only isolation,
at times.

Your voice I could always hear.
Even amongst the quiet clatter or
loud silences
that followed me around.

I never really got too far away.
No matter what I told myself.

For most people,
there isn't love like this.
To most people,
we are anomalies
in a pile of odds and ends.

To me,
there is no pile,
there are no more ends.
Just this beginning.
This something weird.
This something impossible.

*Warning: William did not write or sanction this poem but he did
tell me he liked it.*

White Noise

It's 11:37,
close to midnight,
the TV is on for noise.
It's "white" noise but
it's not white noise.
It doesn't fade
into the background
as we drift to sleep.
Shit maybe it is WHITE noise.
It will keep making itself known.
Periodically waking you up
to tell you it's there.
In some suppressed,
repressed,
racist way.

Racist people
make me sick.
I have
made myself sick.
I have raced people
where the finish line
had room for one.
I have made comments
that were sharpened
on stones
that were thrown in the past

at people who passed
me by
on a lunch break
or a funeral march.
I don't know.
I'm not without guilt.
I'm guilty of hanging around.
I'm not looking
for a jury to hang me.
I don't want
to be a picture on your wall.
The picture of found morality.
I'm not far along.

Really.

I have headphones on
listening to black music
so I don't hear the buzz.
Jamming out
as I work on projects
that are apropos of nothing.
Like myself.
I am still searching for parts
to fix this machine.
The one I was handed.
The one with hands
in everything and
deserving of barely any of it.
What I deserve
was probably already given to me.

I used it and
threw it away.
I'm sure I missed the basket.

It was balled up and
someone
who wished they could have had a shred
of that
had the job
of properly disposing of it.

This planet is fucking stupid.
I say that from a good place.
It's fucking stupid.

There are hundreds
of miles
of food
growing in the ground and
there are people
who fantasize
about the last meal they ate.
Because it was
the last meal they ate and
it was days ago.
People who cry
at night
because the daylight
is where the scars are created
and shown.

Meanwhile,
My white ass is
ranting about how it sucks
when your urologist is hot.

FUCK!
It's a whole thing.
A whole thing
that I have the privilege of thinking.
I have many boxes
checked for me every morning.

Over there,
whereever "there" is,
someone is hurting
because the few boxes they have
are full bullets
in the form of talking points.
Having to say
the same shit
so that the great white Earth
doesn't forget
they need help.
They're happy to help but
they need help.

They need sunshine,
shelter, and a lawn.
Just like me.
They don't want a cross
burning on that lawn.

Just like me.

Except I would think it was prank.
Or a mistake.
Because my shadow
doesn't know hate.

It's black and abstract.
Like the way the world
tries to categorize
whole generations of people.
When I am a part
of generations of people
who owned people,
to make money
that wasn't for the people,
I can't really feel
justice.

I can't be in love with
the status quo.
Especially when the status quo
has never been fair.

So, I stand,
white and ranting,
because privilege catches ears
where other hues are muted,
pleading to nothing.

Because if you're going to care
you already do.
If you have a right to be angry
you already are.
The rest is
the white noise
that put so many to sleep.

MATE
I MADE IT
MALD

Antony Vincent Plocido is a 45-year-old poet from the Twin Cities in Minnesota. He is the author of four other books of poetry: *Sucker Punch Wisdom* – with Jeremy O'Neal & William Peck (2012), *Aging and Other Side Projects* (2016), *Felt this So Many Times* (2018) and the companion book, *The Little Times* (2018). He has also been found in the following collections in *Spectra: Poems of Growth Told Through Chakras* (Err Artist Collective – 2019), *Talking Stick #28* (Jack Pine Press – 2019), *Started by Joy* (2019) and *Martin Lake Journal* (2019).

He is the current Host / Curator of the long running poetry showcase, Poets & Pints. This show takes place every third Wednesday and gives any poet a chance to be featured. The show is typically live from Sisyphus Brewing in Minneapolis but has been made virtual during the pandemic of 2020. For more information please go to:

Facebook: www.facebook.com/groups/poetsandpints

Website: www.crackedwalnut.com/poetsandpints

Tony is also a board member of Cracked Walnut. This is one of the two Twin Cities chapters of The League of MN Poets. Poets & Pints was moved under their umbrella in 2019 (when Tony took over the show) and is now considered their marquee show. However, they do have other monthly shows when then there is no pandemic.

To all of those who were stricken during the COVID-19 pandemic (mentally or physically), Tony hopes that you find hope where you only see strife. Find love in your empty spaces. Find peace while your mind keeps raging.